AMAZING NATIONAL PARKS

ZION National Park

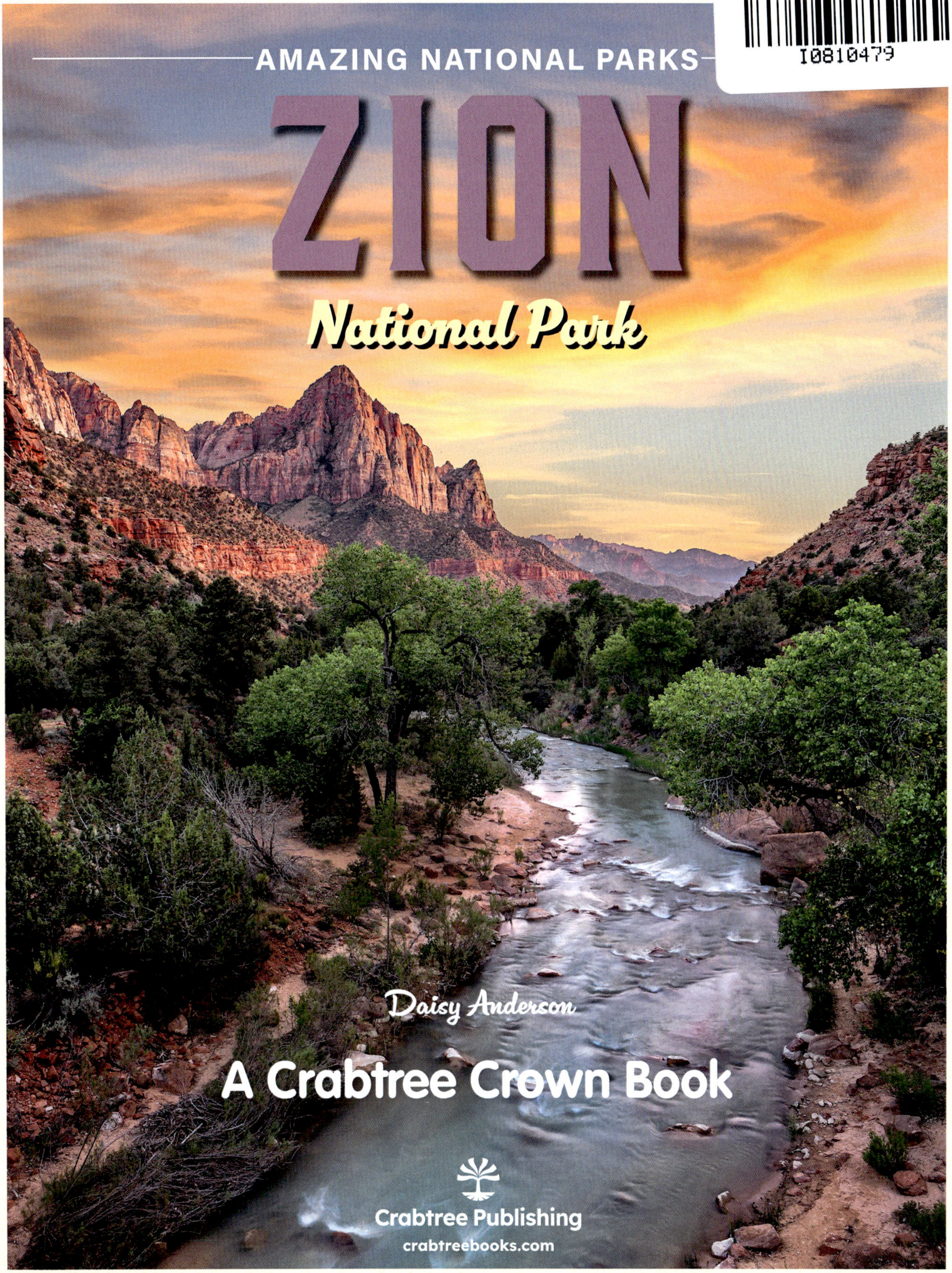

Daisy Anderson

A Crabtree Crown Book

Crabtree Publishing
crabtreebooks.com

School-to-Home Support for Caregivers and Teachers

This appealing book is designed to teach students about core subject areas. Students will build upon what they already know about the subject, and engage in topics that they want to learn more about. Here are a few guiding questions to help readers build their comprehension skills. Possible answers appear here in red.

Before Reading:

What do I know about Zion National Park?

- *I know the national park is in the western United States.*
- *I know many people visit Zion National Park.*

What do I want to learn about this topic?

- *I want to learn what people can see in the national park.*
- *I want to learn what people can do in the national park.*

During Reading:

I'm curious to know...

- *I'm curious to know what kinds of desert animals live in the national park.*
- *I'm curious to know if people can hike through the canyons at the national park.*

How is this like something I already know?

- *I know some snakes live in the desert.*
- *I know that canyons can be very deep.*

After Reading:

What was the author trying to teach me?

- *The author was trying to teach me about why so many people visit Zion National Park.*
- *The author was trying to teach me what visitors can see at the national park.*

How did the photographs and captions help me understand more?

- *The photographs helped me picture what the national park looks like.*
- *The captions gave me extra information about what there is to see at the national park.*

TABLE OF CONTENTS

Chapter 1
Welcome to Zion National Park 4

Chapter 2
The Land and Climate 10

Chapter 3
Plants in the Park 14

Chapter 4
Animals in the Park 18

Chapter 5
Tips on What to See 22

Chapter 6
Tips on What to Do 26

Glossary 30

Index 31

Comprehension Questions 31

About the Author 32

Chapter 1

WELCOME TO ZION NATIONAL PARK

Deep, narrow **canyons** cut through layers of pink and red rock. The Southern Paiute people named this area Mukuntuweap, which means "straight canyon." It was Utah's first national park. Now millions visit Zion National Park every year!

Know the Park

The U.S. government owns national parks and takes care of them. National parks are used to help protect natural areas.

Zion National Park covers 230 square miles (596 square kilometers) in southwestern Utah. The Virgin River flows through the area. The national park has many canyons, but Zion Canyon is the largest. It's 15 miles (24 kilometers) long and almost 3,000 feet (914 meters) deep.

BEFORE IT WAS A PARK

Native American peoples lived in the canyon lands beginning thousands of years ago. The Southern Paiute people settled there more than 800 years ago. They hunted in the canyons and planted crops near the river.

Mormon pioneers arrived in the 1800s. They called the area Zion, the ancient **Hebrew** word for refuge, or safe place. The pioneers pushed the Southern Paiute off their lands. Today, none of the Southern Paiute people live in the national park.

FOUNDING THE PARK

In the early 1900s, the beauty of the area was brought to the attention of President William Howard Taft. He decided it needed to be protected land. He made the area Mukuntuweap National Monument in 1909. It became a national park in 1919 and its name was changed to Zion National Park.

William Howard Taft

THE PARK TODAY

Zion National Park is the 36th-largest national park in the United States. Over 80 percent of the park is a wilderness area. More than 4 million people enjoy Zion National Park every year!

Some wilderness activities, such as overnight backpacking trips, need a permit.

Chapter 2
THE LAND AND CLIMATE

Zion National Park was a fairly flat **basin** 240 million years ago. Streams carried rock and dirt from nearby mountains into the basin where they formed layers of rock over millions of years.

Know the Park

The basin was once covered by a shallow sea. Over time it became a sandy desert. This changing environment is what caused different types of rock to form, which can be seen in the layers in the mountains around the national park.

The rock was **uplifted** into a high **plateau**. Fast-flowing streams and rivers cut through the rock and carved deep, narrow canyons. Today, the Virgin River continues to erode, or wear away, the plateau.

Know the Park

There are many volcanoes in the national park and the area around it. The most recent volcanic eruption inside the area that is now Zion National Park happened about 120,000 years ago.

CLIMATE

Zion's canyon floors are dry desert, but woodlands grow at higher **elevations** where it's cooler. The area around the Virgin River is green with plants that rely on its water.

Many kinds of animals make their homes in the grasses and trees around the river.

Summers in the national park are hot and dry. Summertime temperatures in desert areas often climb above 100 °F (38 °C). Winters are cool, and the tops of the plateaus get wet snow. Spring can bring sudden thunderstorms and flash floods.

Know the Park

Thunderstorms can pop up even on sunny days in Zion. It's wise to keep an eye on the sky and plan to move to higher ground if dark clouds form.

Chapter 3

PLANTS IN THE PARK

The national park has more than 1,000 plant **species**, but pinyon pine and juniper trees cover almost half of the land. These evergreens are found in the canyons between elevations of 4,000 to 8,000 feet (1,219 to 2,438 meters). Ponderosa pine trees cling to sandstone cliffs.

Know the Park

Juniper tree roots can burrow 25 feet (8 meters) down to find water. The trees may live for hundreds of years.

Rabbitbrush is a source of food for animals and provides shelter from the desert heat.

Plants that can survive **drought** are found in the lower parts of the national park. Rabbitbrush blooms with yellow flowers in late summer and early fall. More than 100 kinds of grasses help hold the sandy soil in place.

Fremont cottonwood trees stand tall along the Virgin River. They can grow more than 100 feet (30 meters) high. Willow, ash, and box elder trees also thrive there. Their orange and yellow leaves color the area in the fall.

FLOWERING PLANTS

The national park has the most wildflowers in all of Utah. Many burst into bloom when spring rains come. Western wallflowers color meadows with bright-yellow blossoms. Indian paintbrush plants add a splash of red to the rocks where they grow. Prickly pear cactuses bloom in desert areas.

Chapter 4
ANIMALS IN THE PARK

Zion National Park is full of wildlife. Mule deer, foxes, and rock squirrels make their homes in the park. More than 200 kinds of birds live there, too. The national park's canyons are an important **habitat** for the Mexican spotted owl.

Rock squirrels are often spotted along Riverside Walk trail.

Know the Park

Desert bighorn sheep are most often seen on Zion's east side. They're often on the cliffs, but they do cross the roads, so visitors in cars should keep an eye out.

DESERT BIGHORN SHEEP

Desert bighorn sheep live on rocky cliffs. Their hooves grip the rock, helping them climb quickly to escape mountain lions and other **predators**. Desert bighorn sheep take in **moisture** from the plants they eat and can go days without drinking water.

Collared lizards eat insects, other lizards, and even snakes!

REPTILES

Reptiles love to soak up Zion's heat and are found all over the national park. Sixteen lizard species and 13 kinds of snakes make their homes there. Only one is venomous. The great basin rattlesnake lives in dry, rocky areas and can go for months without water.

Know the Park

Desert tortoises live in the national park but spend most of their lives in underground burrows. Spotting one is a special treat!

WATCHING WILDLIFE

Visitors may see lizards sunning themselves on rocks in the afternoons, but many of the national park's animals are only active in the morning and evening. It's important to remember that all are wild. Keeping your distance and watching through binoculars or by zooming in with your camera is the safest way to enjoy the wildlife.

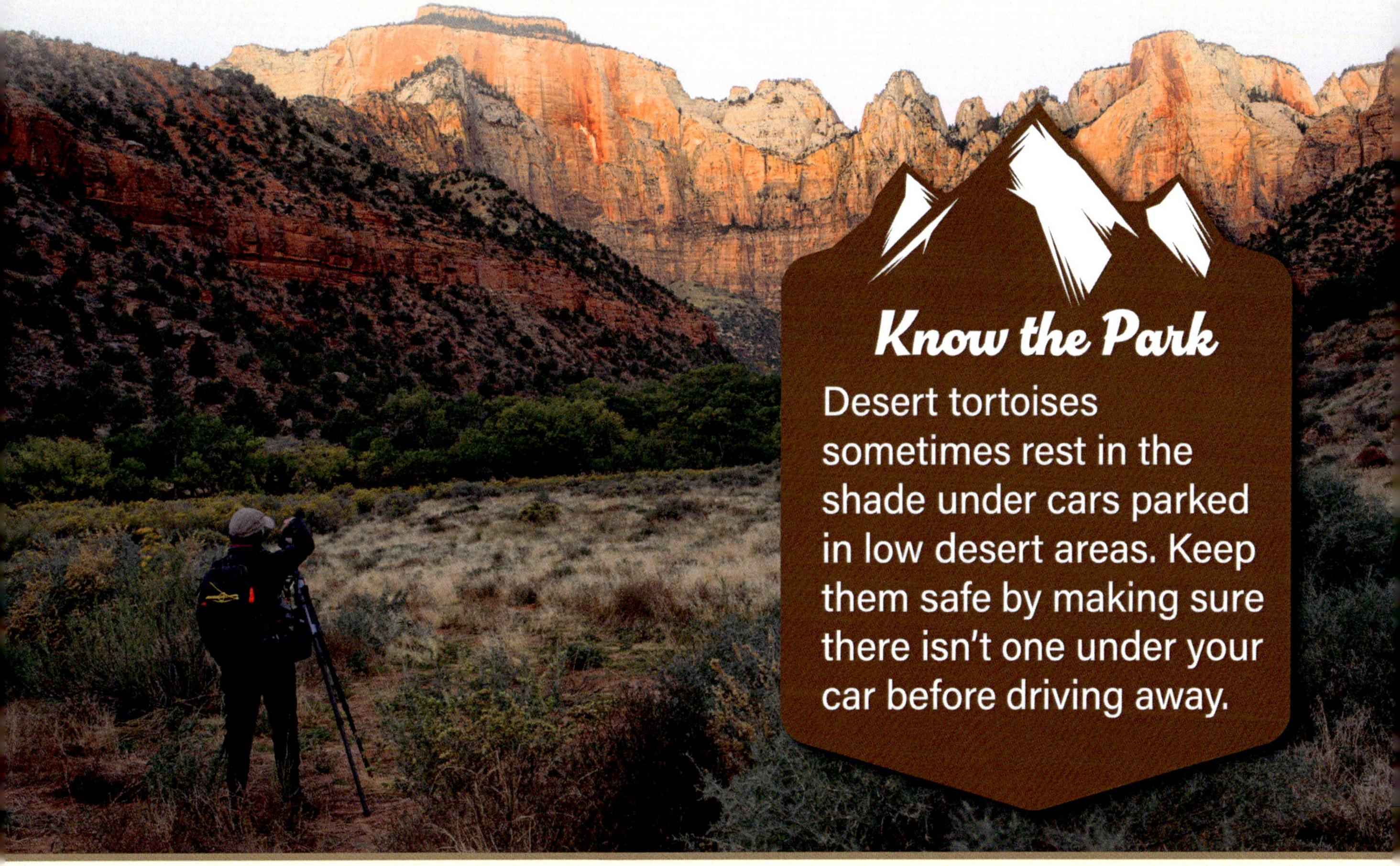

Know the Park

Desert tortoises sometimes rest in the shade under cars parked in low desert areas. Keep them safe by making sure there isn't one under your car before driving away.

Chapter 5
TIPS ON WHAT TO SEE

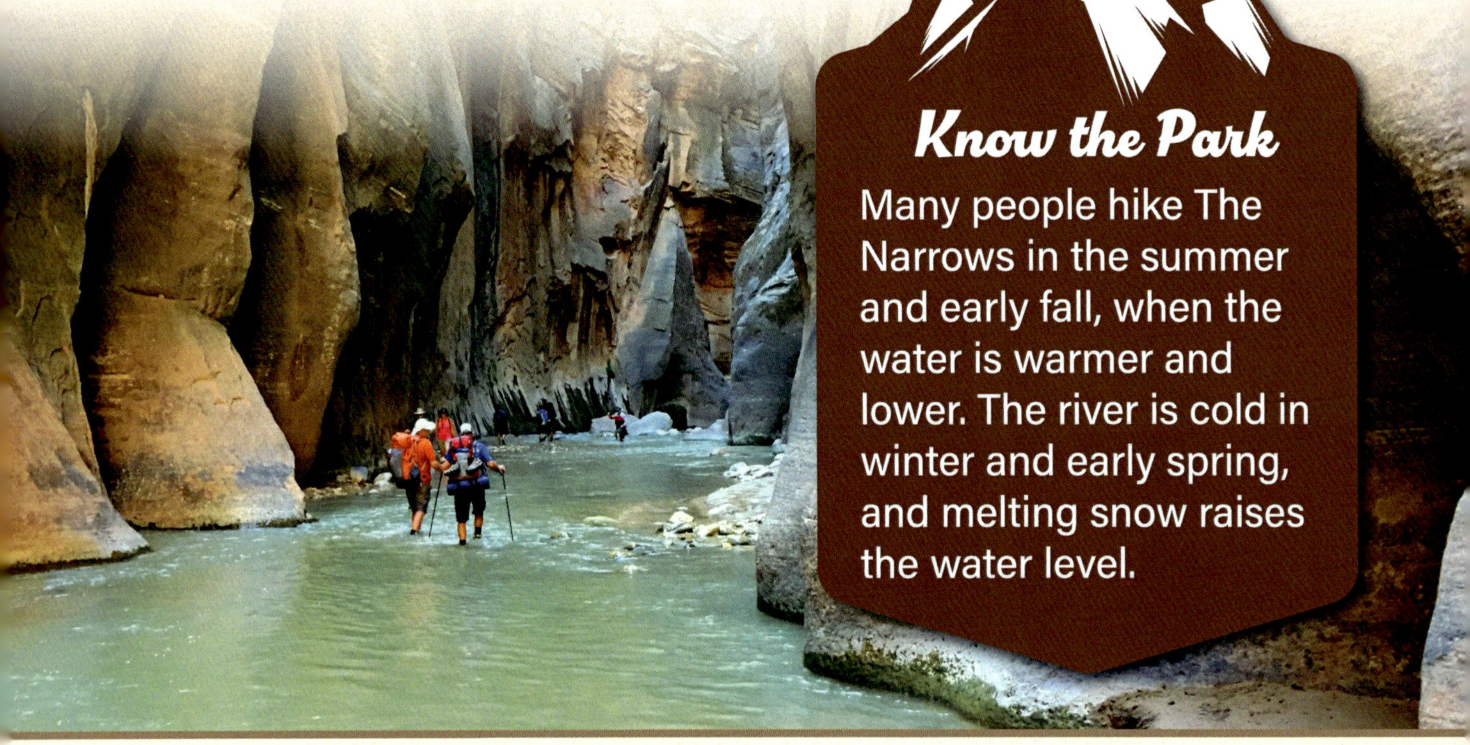

Know the Park
Many people hike The Narrows in the summer and early fall, when the water is warmer and lower. The river is cold in winter and early spring, and melting snow raises the water level.

THE NARROWS

The Narrows, the narrowest part of Zion Canyon, is lined with rock walls that tower 1,000 feet (305 meters) high. Visitors can see The Narrows from the Riverside Walk, a paved trail that's wheelchair friendly. Hikers must walk in the Virgin River to go through The Narrows itself.

Know the Park

The national park is known for areas like Weeping Rock that are called hanging gardens. If you spot flowers and ferns hanging from rocky cliffs, you may be looking at a hanging garden!

WEEPING ROCK

A short trail takes visitors to Weeping Rock. Rain and melting snow on the plateau seep down and make it look as if Weeping Rock is crying. The dripping water allows ferns and flowers to grow on the rock.

Everyone who hikes Angels Landing must have a permit.

ANGELS LANDING

Angels Landing has one of the best views in the national park. This difficult hike takes four or five hours to complete. Sections of the trail are so steep and narrow that hikers hold onto a chain railing to climb it.

ZION CANYON SCENIC DRIVE

A free shuttle bus takes visitors on a 7-mile (11-kilometer) drive through Zion Canyon. Visitors can enjoy the views along the way, and the bus stops at The Narrows, Weeping Rock, Angels Landing, and other popular places in the national park. Hikers can ride the bus to areas where trails begin.

Zion Canyon Scenic Drive closes to cars when the shuttle bus is running.

Chapter 6
TIPS ON WHAT TO DO

Know the Park

Visitors to the national park should follow the Leave No Trace Principles. They include staying on trails, leaving no trash behind, and treating wildlife with respect.

HIKING

Zion National Park has more than 90 miles (145 kilometers) of hiking trails. Some are short and easy. Others, such as Angels Landing, are difficult and go over steep cliffs. The Kolob Canyons trails take hikers into wilderness areas.

Two of Zion's campgrounds are in the desert where summer temperatures reach above 95 °F (35 °C).

CAMPING

Zion has three campgrounds inside park grounds that can be reached by car. More campgrounds are outside the national park but a short drive away. Backpackers can camp in some wilderness areas.

BIKING

Bicycles are allowed on all roads in the park, including Zion Canyon Scenic Drive. You can even load your bike onto the shuttle bus if you don't want to bike back. Bikes can also be ridden on some trails.

Whether you hike, bike, or just drive in for the day, Zion National Park is full of desert beauty!

GLOSSARY

basin (BAY-suhn): A bowl-shaped dip in Earth's surface, where the sides are higher than the bottom

canyons (KAN-yuhnz): Deep valleys with steep sides and often a stream or river running through them

drought (drout): A long period with little or no rain

elevation (el-uh-VAY-shun): The height of a place above sea level

habitat (HAB-i-tat): The place where an animal or plant usually lives

Hebrew (HEE-broo): A language traditionally spoken by people who live or lived in what is now Israel and Palestine

moisture (MOIS-chur): Liquid, such as water, in the form of very small drops

Mormon (MAWR-muhn): A member of a Christian religion that was founded by Joseph Smith in 1830

permit (PUR-mit): An official document that shows a person is allowed to do something

plateau (pla-TOH): An area of flat land that is higher than the land around it

predators (PRED-uh-turz): Animals that hunt other animals for food

species (SPEE-seez): A group of animals or plants that are similar and can reproduce with one another

uplift (UHP-lift): An increase in the vertical elevation of Earth's surface as a result of natural causes

INDEX

Angels Landing 24, 25, 26
biking 28, 29
camping 27
desert bighorn sheep 19
flowering plants 17
hiking 22, 24, 26
reptiles 20
Southern Paiute 4, 6-7
The Narrows 22, 25
Weeping Rock 23, 25
Zion Canyon Scenic Drive 25, 28

COMPREHENSION QUESTIONS

1. Zion National Park is in ____.
   a. Utah
   b. Arizona
   c. Nevada
2. Zion's canyon floors are a ____ region.
   a. woodland
   b. desert
   c. mountain
3. The ____ River runs through the national park.
   a. Rio Grande
   b. Colorado
   c. Virgin
4. True or False: Zion Canyon is the largest canyon in the national park.
5. True or False: There are no trees in Zion because the national park is in the desert.

Answers: 1. A, 2. B, 3. C, 4. True, 5. False

ABOUT THE AUTHOR

Daisy Anderson loves to write real-life books for curious kids. She lives in the Midwest, where she enjoys exploring the great outdoors with her two dogs. When Daisy isn't writing, she's out hiking and having fun in nature.

Written by: Daisy Anderson
Designed by: Bobbie Houser
Series Development: James Earley
Proofreader: Melissa Boyce
Educational Consultant: Marie Lemke M.Ed.
Production manager: Candice Campbell

Photographs:
t = Top, c = Center, b = Bottom, l = Left, r = Right
Alamy: INTERFOTO: p. 6; Old Books Images: p. 7; Alpha Historica: p. 8 t
Library of Congress: p. 8 b
Shutterstock: anthony heflin: cover, p. 1; Fotos593: p. 4; Kris Wiktor: p. 5 t; Rainer Lesniewski: p. 5 b; Maridav: p. 9; photozims: p. 10-11; warasit phothisuk: p. 12; p. 13; Allison Herreid: p. 14; Kelly vanDellen: p. 15; Bill45: p. 16, 21; urosr: p. 17; RMF: p. 18 tr; Tami Freed: p. 18 br; Eddys Photo Shop: p. 18 br; Brian A Wolf: p. 19; Sholmes370: p. 20; SWMC: p. 22; fabernova: p. 23; evenfh: p. 24; OLOS: p. 25; Allen.G: p. 26; Andriy Blokhin: p. 27; Jim Parkin: p. 28; Mark Muratore: p. 29

Crabtree Publishing

crabtreebooks.com 800-387-7650

Printed in the U.S.A./CP2025

Published in Canada
Crabtree Publishing
616 Welland Ave.
St. Catharines, Ontario
L2M 5V6

Published in the United States
Crabtree Publishing
347 Fifth Ave
Suite 1402-145
New York, NY 10016

Library and Archives Canada Cataloguing in Publication
Available at Library and Archives Canada

Library of Congress Cataloging-in-Publication Data
Available at the Library of Congress

Hardcover: 978-1-0398-6487-0
Paperback: 978-1-0398-6556-3
Ebook (pdf): 978-1-0398-6625-6
Epub: 978-1-0398-6694-2